KU-130-407

Orders: Please contact How2become Ltd, Suite 2, 50 Churchill Square Business Centre, Kings Hill, Kent ME19 4YU.

You can order through Amazon.co.uk under ISBN 9781910602492, via the website www.How2Become.com or through Gardners.com.

ISBN: 9781910602492

First published in 2015 by How2become Ltd.

Typeset for How2become Ltd by Anton Pshinka.

Printed in Great Britain for How2become Ltd by: CMP (uk) Limited, Poole, Dorset.

Disclaimer

Every effort has been made to ensure that the information contained within this guide is accurate at the time of publication. How2become Ltd are not responsible for anyone failing any part of any selection process as a result of the information contained within this guide. How2become Ltd and their authors cannot accept any responsibility for any errors or omissions within this guide, however caused. No responsibility for loss or damage occasioned by any person acting, or refraining from action, as a result of the material in this publication can be accepted by How2become Ltd.

The information within this guide does not represent the views of any third party service or organisation.

MATHS

Please <u>DO NOT</u> write answers on this book

THE
REVISION
SERIES

www.How2Become.com

As part of this product you have also received FREE access to online tests that will help you to pass Key Stage 2 MATHS *(Data and Statistics)*.

To gain access, simply go to:

www.PsychometricTestsOnline.co.uk

Get more products for passing any test at:

www.how2become.com

CONTENTS

THE
REVISION
SERIES

INTERPRETING
DATA

INTERPRETING DATA

WHAT IS DATA?

DATA ⟹ INFORMATION

In order to make information easier to understand, the information is often put in graphs, charts or tables.

When it comes to data, there are two main areas that you should focus on:

- Collecting and Recording Data;
- Interpreting Data.

COLLECTING AND RECORDING DATA

- Collecting and recording data requires YOU to read the data and collect all the information in order to record the results.
- The data collected can be recorded by a number of different methods. There are many graphs and charts that you are expected to learn and be able to use, and this guide will show you how to use each type of graph, chart or table.

INTERPRETING DATA

- Interpreting data requires you to look at the data in the graph, chart or table, and analyse what the data is showing.
- By putting the data into these graphs/charts, you are clearly able to see data differences and similarities, you are able to spot patterns, and you are able to work out the **mean**, **mode**, **median** and **range** of sets of data (these terms will be discussed in the next chapter).

TYPES OF DATA

Tables	Tallies and Frequencies	Bar Charts	Pie Charts
Line Graphs	Pictograms	Carroll Diagrams	Venn Diagrams

On the next few pages, we have provided examples of the common types of graphs or charts that you will be working with.

TABLES – *Examples*

	Train 1	Train 2	Train 3	Train 4
Petersberg	6.45	7.04	-------	8.04
Hammersmith	7.00	-------	7.45	8.19
St Leonard's Station	7.12	7.20	8.00	-------
Mariweather	7.36	7.42	-------	8.30
Goldsberg	7.52	-------	8.19	8.48
Upperside	8.12	8.04	8.27	9.04
Franks Park	8.30	8.27	8.48	9.28

	Test 1	Test 2
Katie	33	38
Matt	42	48
Simon	18	19
John	9	21
Rose	32	38
Scarlett	31	21
James	35	19

	Cats	Dogs	Rabbits	Other
Scarlett	--------	--------	--------	--------
Freddie	--------	--------	--------	--------
Preston	--------	--------	--------	--------
Anil	--------	--------	--------	--------

- ❖ Scarlett = 2 cats, 1 dog
- ❖ Preston = 1 cat, 1 dog and 2 others
- ❖ Freddie = 3 rabbits
- ❖ Anil = None

TALLIES AND FREQUENCIES – *Examples*

Pets	Tally	Total
Cats	⦀⦀ ⦀⦀ |	11
Dogs	⦀⦀ ⦀⦀ ||	12
Hamsters	⦀⦀ |	6
Guinea pigs	||	2
Rabbits	||||	4
Other	⦀⦀ ⦀⦀ ⦀⦀ ||||	19

BAR CHARTS – *Examples*

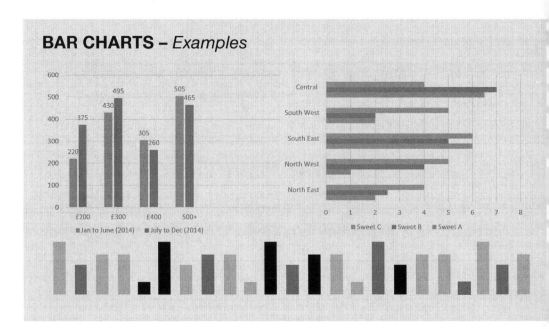

PIE CHARTS – *Examples*

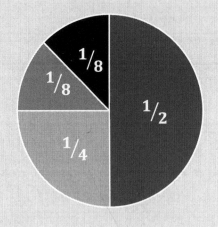

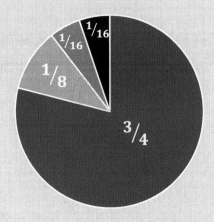

LINE GRAPHS – *Examples*

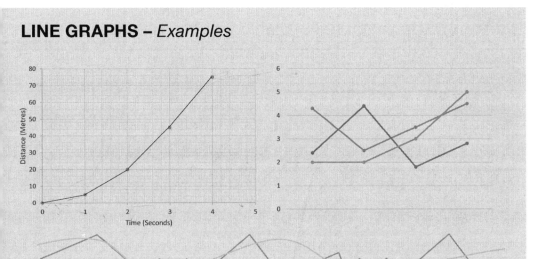

CARROLL DIAGRAMS – *Examples*

	Multiples of 3	Factors of 32
ODD	3 9 15 21	1
EVEN	6 30 18 12	2 32 8 4 16

VENN DIAGRAMS – *Examples*

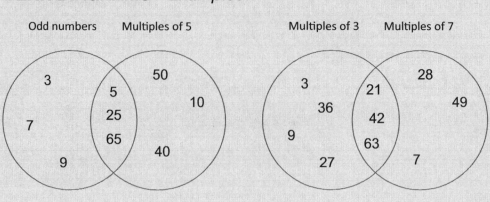

HOW TO USE THIS GUIDE

This guide is formatted in an easy and clear structure so that you can make the most out of your practice guide.

Each chapter focuses on a particular graph, chart or table.

I recommend that you practice ALL of the questions contained within this guide. This will give you a better understanding of what to expect in your Maths exams.

Each chapter contains the following:

- Information regarding each type of chart;
- Example questions;
- Practice questions;
- Detailed answers and explanations.

Now move on to the practice questions!

THE
REVISION
SERIES

MEAN, MODE, MEDIAN AND RANGE

MEAN, MODE, MEDIAN AND RANGE

Mode, mean and *median* are TYPES of average.

Range is the DIFFERENCE between the smallest number and the biggest number.

> **MEAN** ⟹ the total of the numbers DIVIDED by how many numbers there are.

Example 1

4   6   11   20   18   1

Step 1 = add up all of the numbers = 4 + 6 + 11 + 20 + 18 + 1 = 60.

Step 2 = divide it by how many numbers there are (6).

$60 \div 6 = 10$

Step 3 = so the mean number of this set of data is 10.

Example 2

9   15   31   6   24   5

Step 1 = add up all of the numbers = 9 + 15 + 31 + 6 + 24 + 5 = 90.

Step 2 = divide it by how many numbers there are (6).

$90 \div 6 = 15$

Step 2 = so the mean number of this set of data is 15.

> **MODE** ⟹ the value that appears the MOST.

Example 1

7   9   5   7   2   1   3   6

Step 1 = you need to find the number that occurs the most number of times.

Step 2 = the value '7' occurs twice. No other number occurs more, so this is the correct answer.

REMEMBER = **MO**DE equals **MO**ST.

MEAN, MODE, MEDIAN AND RANGE

MEDIAN ⟹ the median is the MIDDLE number.

Example 1

7   3   1   11   18   14

Step 1 = first you need to rearrange the numbers from smallest to biggest:

1   3   7   11   14   18

Step 2 = now you need to work out which number is in the middle.

Step 3 = sometimes you might have two numbers in the middle (as demonstrated in this example). All you have to do is add up both the middle numbers and divide the answer by 2.

7 + 11 (the numbers in the middle) = 18 ÷ 2 = 9.

Step 4 = so 9 is the median of this set of data.

RANGE ⟹ the difference between the biggest and the smallest number.

Example 1

5   16   4   18   16   21

Step 1 = find the smallest number (4).

Step 2 = find the biggest number = (21).

Step 3 = subtract the smallest number from the biggest number:

21 − 4 = 17.

Step 4 = so 17 is the range of this set of data.

Question 1

Below is a set of numbers.

11 8 24 16 4 3 4 1 12 7

a) What is the **mean** of this set of data?

b) What is the **mode** of this set of data?

c) What is the **range** of this set of data?

d) What is the **median** of this set of data?

Question 2

Below is a set of numbers.

6 9 3 2 6 8 7 3 11 15

a) What is the **mean** of this set of data?

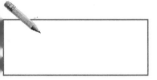

b) What is the **mode** of this set of data?

c) What is the **range** of this set of data?

d) What is the **median** of this set of data?

Question 3

Freddie goes to the grocery store. He is looking over his receipt.

RECEIPT

Bread	£1.25
Bottle of coke	£1.00
Bar of chocolate	£1.99
Eggs	£0.89
Tomatoes	£1.75
Tins of soup	£3.25
DVD	£4.87

a) What was the **mean** amount spent by Freddie? To 2 decimal places.

b) Work out the **range** of the prices.

Question 4

Below are three empty boxes. Write three **different** numbers so that the **mean** of the three numbers is **9**.

Question 5

Scarlett and Lalita both run 100 metres 10 times. Their times are recorded below (in seconds).

SCARLETT'S TIMES		
12.4	11.9	12.9
13.4	13.8	14.2
13.4	15.1	13.7
	12.9	

LALITA'S TIMES		
15.4	13.2	16.4
12.7	12.9	16.1
13.6	13.2	11.5
	12.5	

a) What is Lalita's **mean** time?

b) What is the **range** between Scarlett's fastest time, and Lalita's slowest time?

c) What is the **median** time for Scarlett?

d) Work out the **mode** of Lalita's times.

ANSWERS TO MEAN, MODE, MEDIAN AND RANGE

Q1. a) 9

EXPLANATION = to work out the mean:

$11 + 8 + 24 + 16 + 4 + 3 + 4 + 1 + 12 + 7 = 90$

$90 \div 10 = 9$

b) 4

EXPLANATION = to work out the mode, you need to work out what number occurs the most. The number '4' occurs twice. No other number occurs more times, therefore this is the correct answer.

c) 23

EXPLANATION = to work out the range:

(Biggest number) – (Smallest number) $= 24 - 1 = 23$

d) 7.5

EXPLANATION = to work out the median:

The numbers in ascending order are: 1, 3, 4, 4, 7, 8, 11, 12, 16 and 24

The numbers 7 and 8 are both in the middle. So, $7 + 8 = 15$

$15 \div 2 = 7.5$

Q2. a) 7

EXPLANATION = to work out the mean:

$6 + 9 + 3 + 2 + 6 + 8 + 7 + 3 + 11 + 15 = 70$

$70 \div 10 = 7$

b) 6 and 3

EXPLANATION = to work out the mode, you need to work out what number occurs the most. The numbers 6 and 3 both occur twice, therefore these would both be the correct answer.

c) 13

EXPLANATION = to work out the range:

(Biggest number) – (Smallest number) $= 15 - 2 = 13$

d) 6.5

EXPLANATION = to work out the median:

The numbers in ascending order are: 2, 3, 3, 6, 6, 7, 8, 9, 11 and 15

The numbers 6 and 7 are both in the middle. So, 6 + 7 = 13

13 ÷ 2 = 6.5

Q3. a) £2.14

EXPLANATION = 1.25 + 1.00 + 1.99 + 0.89 + 1.75 + 3.25 + 4.87 = 15.00

15.00 ÷ 7 = 2.1428. To 2 decimal places = 2.14

b) £3.98

EXPLANATION = to work out the range:

(Biggest number) – (Smallest number) = 4.87 – 0.89 = 3.98

Q4. 8, 5 and 14 (*Please note, you could have used any three DIFFERENT numbers, so long as the numbers add up to 27*).

EXPLANATION = the mean of the 3 numbers needs to be 9. Therefore 9 x 3 = 27. (The 3 numbers all need to add up to 27. Once added up to 27, you can divide it by how many numbers there are, which is 3, and you will reach the mean number of 9).

Q5. a) 13.75

EXPLANATION = Lalita's mean time = 15.4 + 13.2 + 16.4 + 12.7 + 12.9 + 16.1 + 13.6 + 13.2 + 11.5 + 12.5 = 137.5

137.5 ÷ 10 = 13.75

b) 4.5

EXPLANATION = Scarlett's fastest time = 11.9. Lalita's slowest time = 16.4

To work out the range = 16.4 – 11.9 = 4.5

c) 13.4

EXPLANATION = to work out the median time for Scarlett:

The numbers in ascending order are: 11.9, 12.4, 12.9, 12.9, 13.4, 13.4, 13.7, 13.8, 14.2 and 15.1

The numbers in the middle are 13.4 and 13.4, therefore 13.4 is the median time.

d) 13.2

EXPLANATION = to work out the mode, you need to work out what number occurs the **most**. For Lalita's times, the number 13.2 occurs twice, and therefore this is the correct answer.

HOW ARE YOU GETTING ON?

THE
REVISION
SERIES

TABLES

TABLES

Tables are a GREAT way to make things easier to read.

They are used to write down data about different things.

Example

How children get to school	Number of pupils
Walking	27
Car	34
Cycle	16
Bus	18
Train	3
Taxi	2
TOTAL	**100**

The **headings** tell us what the data is referring to in each column.

The **total** tells us how many people took part in the study.

To find out how many people walk to school, you would look at the row that says 'Walking' and then read the number of pupils in that same row (which is 27).

TABLES

DIFFERENT TYPES OF TABLES

There are different types of tables depending on what the data is referring to. However, if you learn how to read tables correctly, you will be able to apply the same method to ANY table.

Types of tables that you should learn:

- Two-way tables
- Distance tables
- Timetables

TWO-WAY TABLES

Two-way tables show two sets of data.

Subheadings for two different groups.

Subheadings for two different groups.

	Boys	Girls
Class A	12	16
Class B	21	13

You can read the table in rows (This shows the TOTAL number of boys AND girls in CLASS A).

You can read the table in columns (This shows the TOTAL number of BOYS in BOTH classes).

TABLES

DISTANCE TABLES

Distance tables only use ONE set of headings. They show the distance between different places.

	Place A		
Place B		13	
Place C	21	23	
Place D	6	15	35

What is the distance from Place A to Place D?

Step 1 = find Place A on the table.
Step 2 = work your way down the column (of Place A), until you reach the row that says (Place D).
Step 2 = the arrows on the diagram show you how to work it out.
Step 3 = the distance from Place A to Place D is 35.

TIMETABLES

If you catch a train or a bus, you are often required to read the timetable to know when the bus or train is arriving.

Timetables are an easy way of looking at lots of different times including departure and arrival times.

Stockett Lane	13:27	13:42	13:52
Loose Road	14:00	14:15	14:32
Grove Road	14:12	14:29	14:49
High Street	14:38	14:53	15:06

Tip 1 = Make sure you know what COLUMNS are, and what ROWS are. Remember columns go downwards, and rows go across.

Tip 2 = Drawing arrows can help you to identify what column and row you are working with.

REMEMBER = in a timetable, if there is a number missing (usually filled in with a dotted line) that means the train or bus does not stop there).

Question 1

Below is a table of all the pets that each child has owned in their lifetime.

Names	Dog	Cat	Fish	Bird	Rabbit	Other
Yolanda	1	-	3	-	-	2
Anil	3	-	-	-	1	-
Emma	-	2	2	-	2	-
Gareth	-	-	7	8	-	2
Ross	2	3	9	-	1	-
Marcus	1	-	3	1	-	1
Stacey	2	1	6	-	4	3

a) Who has owned the most number of pets in their lifetime?

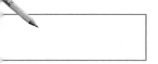

b) What is the mean number of total pets owned by everyone?

Question 2

Here is part of a train timetable.

	Stop A	Stop B	Stop C
Train 1	07:15	08:32	08:55
Train 2	08:05	09:22	09:45

In hours and minutes, how long does it take Train 1 to get from Stop A to Stop B?

Question 3

Study the train times below, and answer the following questions.

	Train 1	Train 2	Train 3	Train 4
Petersberg	06:45	07:04	------	08:04
Hammersmith	07:00	-------	07:45	08:19
St Leonard's Station	07:12	07:20	08:00	-------
Mariweather	07:36	07:42	------	08:30
Goldsberg	07:52	-------	08:19	08:48
Upperside	08:12	08:04	08:27	09:04
Franks Park	08:30	08:27	08:48	09:28

a) If I were leaving from Hammersmith, what train time is best to catch if I wish to arrive in Franks Park just before 9 o'clock? <u>Please circle your answer.</u>

A	B	C	D
7.04	8.04	7.45	7.00

b) How many minutes slower does the 07:36 train from Mariweather take to get to Upperside, compared to the 07:42 train from Mariweather?

Question 4

Freddie needs your help! Below is a distance table. It shows the number of miles between different places. Freddie wants to work out the distance, in miles, from Bewl Down to Prim East.

DISTANCE TABLE			Sand Stone
		Bewl Down	75
	Eden Head	54	81
Prim East	63	96	84

Question 5

Below is a table which shows the cost of train fares to different places (boarding from the same place).

		Maidstone	Canterbury	Dover
CHILD	Single	£7.60	£9.40	£11.90
	Return	£13.20	£17.50	£20.30
ADULT	Single	£13.20	£19.60	£21.70
	Return	£24.00	£35.10	£39.80

a) What is the difference in return tickets for a child ticket, compared to an adult ticket to Canterbury?

b) What is the total cost for two adult singles, and three child singles to Dover? Please write down your calculations.

c) How much more does it cost four adults to travel to Dover than to Maidstone? (Both on a single ticket). Please write down your calculations.

ANSWERS TO TABLES

Q1. a) Gareth

EXPLANATION = to work out the number of total pets owned by each child, you need to add up each row.

Gareth has owned a total of 17 pets. No other person has owned more pets, so Gareth is the correct answer.

b) 10

EXPLANATION = to work out the mean number of pets owned by everyone, first add up the total number of pets, and then divide it by the number of people.

$6 + 4 + 6 + 17 + 15 + 6 + 16 = 70$

$70 \div 7 = 10$

So the mean total is 10.

Q2. 1 hour and 17 minutes

EXPLANATION = Train 1 leaves Stop A at 07:15 and arrives at Stop B at 08:32.

07:15 (add 45 minutes = 08:00)

08:00 (add 32 minutes = 08:32)

$45 + 32 = 77$ minutes.

REMEMBER = the question asks for the answer in hours and minutes, so 77 minutes converted into hours and minutes = 1 hour and 17 minutes.

Q3. a) C = 7:45

EXPLANATION = if you wanted to arrive in Franks Park before 09:00, you need to read the row that is for Franks Park and see which time is closest to 09:00. This would be '08:48'. Now read up this column until you reach the column Hammersmith, and this will be 07:45.

b) 14 minutes slower

EXPLANATION = first work out how long it takes for the 07:36 train. You arrive in Upperside at 08:12.

07:36 (add 24 minutes = 08:00)

08:00 (add 12 minutes = 08:12). So this train takes $24 + 12 = 36$ minutes.

The 07:42 train arrives at Upperside at 08:04.

       07:42 (add 18 minutes = 08:00)

       08:00 (add 4 minutes = 08:04). So this train takes 18 + 4 = 22 minutes.

Therefore the first train is 36 – 22 = 14 minutes slower.

Q4. 96 miles

EXPLANATION = you should read the distance table like so:

DISTANCE TABLE			Sand Stone
		Bewl Down	75
	Eden Head	54	81
Prim East	63	96	84

Q5. a) £17.60

EXPLANATION = child return ticket to Canterbury = £17.50

Adult return ticket to Canterbury = £35.10

So the difference between these prices = 35.10 – 17.50 = 17.60

    b) £79.10

EXPLANATION = 2 adult singles to Dover = 21.70 x 2 = 43.40

3 children singles to Dover = 11.90 x 3 = 35.70

Total cost = 43.40 + 35.70 = 79.10

    c) £34.00

EXPLANATION = 4 adult single tickets to Dover = 21.70 x 4 = 86.80

4 adult single tickets to Maidstone = 13.20 x 4 = 52.80

86.80 – 52.80 = 34.00

HOW ARE YOU GETTING ON?

TALLIES
AND
FREQUENCIES

TALLIES AND FREQUENCIES

UNDERSTANDING TALLIES

Tallies are a GREAT way to help you keep count.

Tally marks will look like this:

| | || ||| |||| 卌 ∘∘○

1   2   3   4   5

> Once you get to 4, the next tally mark will cross off the 4 marks (to make 5). This makes it easier to count the totals.

You can record this information using a tally and frequency graph.

Colours	Tally	Frequency
Pink	卌 卌 卌 |||	18
Blue	卌 卌	10
Red	卌 ||||	9
Orange	卌 ||	7
Green	卌 卌 ||	12

FREQUENCY is another word for TOTAL. These tables can be referred to as frequency tables.

Now you try!

Fill in the tally chart using the frequencies shown.

Pets	Tally	Frequency
Dogs		7
Cats		13
Rabbits		19
Guinea Pigs		21
Fish		3

Question 1

Below is a list of how 24 children travel to school. Use the data below and organise it in the tally and frequency diagram below. The first tally has been done for you.

Walk Cycle Walk Bus Bus Car Walk Train Taxi Car Walk Bus

Bus Walk Car Car Car Taxi Train Walk Walk Bus Bus Car

Transport	Tally	Frequency
Walk	|	
Bus		
Car		
Train		
Cycle		
Taxi		
TOTAL	24	24

Question 2

Below is an incomplete tally graph of the number of vegetable sales in an hour. Complete the table.

Vegetables	Tally	Frequency
Carrots	卌 卌 卌 |||	
Potatoes	卌 卌	
Broccoli		9
Brussels	卌 ||	
Green Beans		12

Question 3

Freddie VS *Preston*

Below is a record of the number of crimes that each superhero has prevented in one week. Each small image of the character represents one crime. Fill in the tally chart.

Superhero	Tally	Frequency
Freddie		
Preston		

Question 4

Below is a tally chart of a pie eating contest, and the number of times each person won.

Name	Tally	Frequency
Jamie	ЖЖ ЖЖ II	12
Lucas	ЖЖ II	7
Nathan	III	3
Timmy	ЖЖ I	6
Marvin	ЖЖ III	8

a) How many pie eating contests were there in total?

b) How many more pie eating contests did Jamie win than Timmy?

Question 5

15 pupils took a spelling test. Test scores were out of 50. The tally graph below is incomplete. Fill in the tally graph using the test scores below.

| 25 | 32 | 27 | 19 | 40 | 34 | 46 | 27 | 13 | 28 | 40 | 39 | 25 | 35 | 23 |

Test Score	Number of pupils (Tally)
0 - 10	
11- 20	
21 – 30	
31 – 40	
41 - 50	

ANSWERS TO TALLIES AND FREQUENCIES

Q1. Your answer should look like this:

Transport	Tally	Frequency
Walk	$\cancel{||||}$ ||	7
Bus	$\cancel{||||}$		6
Car	$\cancel{||||}$		6
Train	||	2
Cycle			1
Taxi	||	2
TOTAL	24	24

Q2. Your answer should look like this:

Vegetables	Tally	Frequency
Carrots	$\cancel{||||}$ $\cancel{||||}$ $\cancel{||||}$ |||	18
Potatoes	$\cancel{||||}$ $\cancel{||||}$	10
Broccoli	$\cancel{||||}$ ||||	9
Brussels	$\cancel{||||}$ ||	7
Green Beans	$\cancel{||||}$ $\cancel{||||}$ ||	12

Q3. Your answer should look like this:

Superhero	Tally	Frequency
Freddie	JHT JHT	10
Preston	JHT JHT I	11

Q4. a) 36

EXPLANATION = add up all of the frequencies:

12 + 7 + 3 + 6 + 8 = 36

b) 6

EXPLANATION = Jamie won 12 pie eating contests, and Timmy won 6. Therefore, Jamie won 6 more contests.

Q5. Your answer should look like this:

Test Score	Number of pupils (Tally)
0 - 10	
11- 20	II
21 – 30	JHT I
31 – 40	JHT I
41 - 50	I

HOW ARE YOU GETTING ON?

THE
REVISION
SERIES

BAR
CHARTS

BAR CHARTS

Bar charts are SIMPLE and EASY!

They allow you to compare lots of information by laying out the results in a simple and easy to read format.

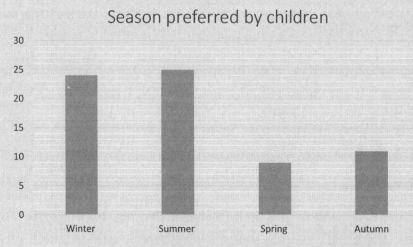

Season preferred by children

The shaded rectangles on the bar chart are called 'bars'.

If there is no bar, that means no person chose that answer.

To read the bar chart, look at the bar that the question is referring to, read up until it reaches the line. Read along and see what number it shows.

Which season is most popular?

Step 1 = to see which season is most popular, you can quickly work out the answer by seeing which bar is the highest. In this case, summer is the most popular.

How many people chose winter as their favourite season?

Step 1 = look at the bar for winter.
Step 2 = read up until where the bar finishes.
Step 3 = read across and see which number it is.
Step 3 = 24 people chose winter.

BAR CHARTS

Bar charts can also be drawn SIDEWAYS.

You read these bar charts exactly the same. But instead of reading the bars vertically, you will read them horizontally.

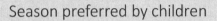

Season preferred by children

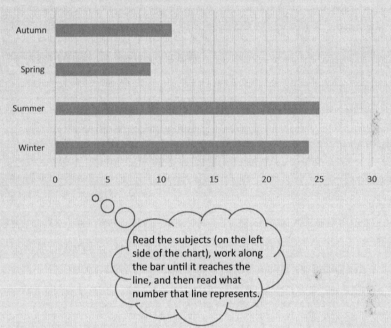

Read the subjects (on the left side of the chart), work along the bar until it reaches the line, and then read what number that line represents.

Now you try!

Using the above bar chart, how many more people chose summer over autumn?

How many people chose spring as their favourite season?

Question 1

Below is a bar chart of 100 pupils' favourite takeaway food.

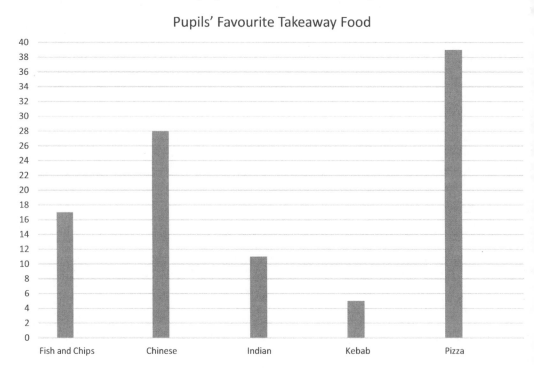

Pupils' Favourite Takeaway Food

a) What percentage of pupils liked Chinese the most?

b) What was the range of the most popular takeaway and the least favourite takeaway?

c) How many pupils' favourite takeaway was pizza?

Question 2

Temperatures were recorded for a week. Use these results and fill in the bar chart below.

DAY	TEMPERATURE
Monday	11°C
Tuesday	6°C
Wednesday	9°C
Thursday	8°C
Friday	4°C
Saturday	21°C
Sunday	7°C

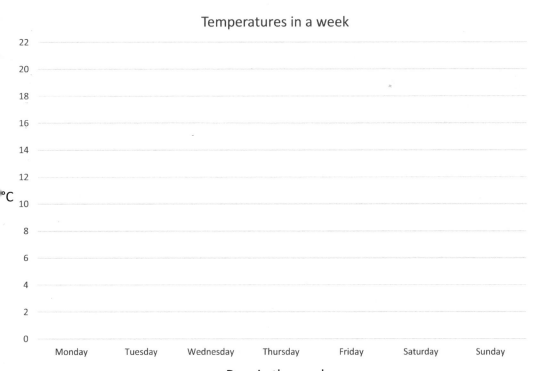

Temperatures in a week

Question 3

Below is a bar chart illustrating children's favourite breakfasts.

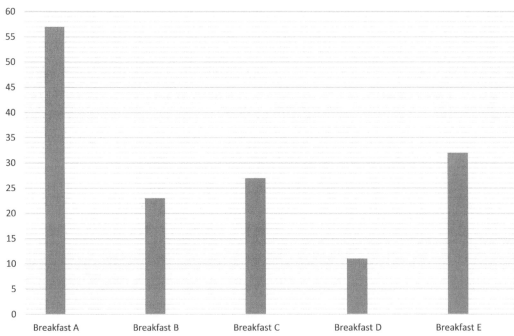

Pupils' Favourite Breakfasts

a) How many people took part in the survey?

b) How many more people preferred Breakfast A to Breakfast C?

c) What is the mean number of this set of data?

Question 4

Freddie needs your help. He wants to put the information from his tally into a bar chart. Can you do this for him?

Genre of Films	Tally
Romance	JHT JHT JHT III
Comedy	JHT JHT II
Action	JHT JHT JHT IIII
Horror	JHT III
Fantasy	JHT JHT III

Favourite Films

Number of people

22
20
18
16
14
12
10
8
6
4
2
0

Romance   Comedy   Action   Horror   Fantasy

Genre of Films

Question 5

Below is a bar chart of favourite sports, recorded for both boys and girls.

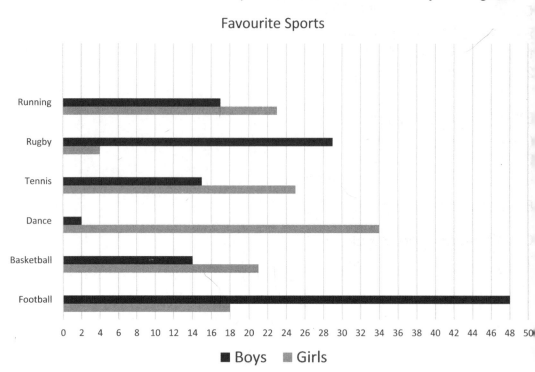

Favourite Sports

a) How many boys chose basketball as their favourite sport?

b) How many people took part in this survey altogether?

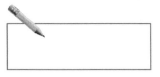

c) What is the difference between the number of girls who choose running, compared to the number of boys?

ANSWERS TO BAR CHARTS

Q1. a) 28%

EXPLANATION = the survey was of 100 people. 28 pupils' favourite takeaway food was Chinese. Therefore this is 28% of 100(%).

b) 34

EXPLANATION = to work out the range:

(Most popular takeaway) – (Least favourite takeaway) =

Pizza – Kebab = 39 – 5 = 34

c) 39

EXPLANATION = 39 people chose pizza as their favourite takeaway.

Q2. Your bar chart should look something like this:

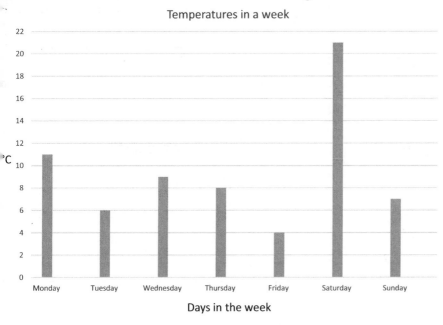

Q3. a) 150

EXPLANATION = add up all of the bars = 57 + 23 + 27 + 11 + 32 = 150

b) 30

EXPLANATION = the number of people who liked Breakfast A = 57. The number of people who liked Breakfast C = 27

So 30 more people preferred Breakfast A compared to Breakfast C.

c) 30

EXPLANATION = the total of this set of data = 150. There are 5 columns. So, 150 ÷ 5 = 30. So the mean number of this set of data is 30.

Q4. Your bar chart should look something like this:

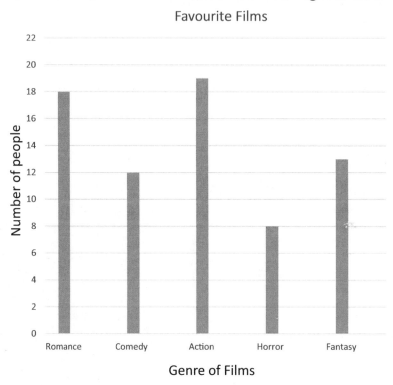

Favourite Films

Q5. a) 14

EXPLANATION = 14 boys chose basketball as their favourite sport.

b) 250

EXPLANATION = 125 girls took part in the survey, and 125 boys. So, 125 + 125 = 250

c) 6

EXPLANATION = the number of girls who chose running as their favourite sport = 23. The number of boys who chose running as their favourite sport = 17. So the difference is = 23 − 17 = 6

HOW ARE YOU GETTING ON?

THE
REVISION
SERIES

PIE
CHARTS

PIE CHARTS

PIE CHARTS AND PROPORTIONS

Pie charts are another useful way of displaying data.

They are named 'pie' charts because they kind of look like a pie!

They show data as proportions. The size of each segment (slice) tells you how much each segment is worth.

FAVOURITE THING ABOUT SNOW

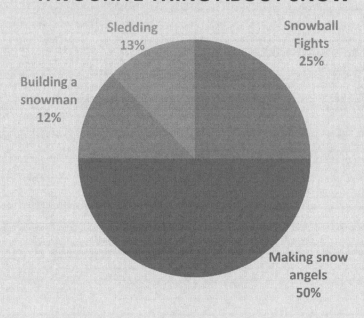

In ANY pie chart, the percentages need to add up to 100%.
In ANY pie chart, the fractions need to add up to 1.

Question

If 60 people took part in the survey above, how many people chose snowball fights as their favourite thing about snow?

Step 1 = 60 (total number of people) ÷ 100 (%) x 25 (% of people who chose snowball fights) = 15.

Step 2 = so 15 people chose snowball fights.

Question 1

Below is a pie chart.

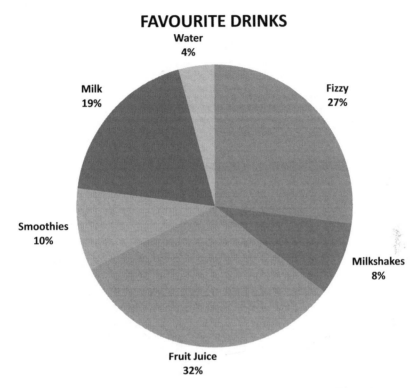

FAVOURITE DRINKS

Water 4%
Milk 19%
Fizzy 27%
Smoothies 10%
Milkshakes 8%
Fruit Juice 32%

a) Fizzy drinks are more popular than fruit juice. True or false?

b) What percentage of people chose smoothies as their favourite drink?

c) If 100 people took part in this survey, how many people chose milk as their favourite drink?

Question 2

Freddie is struggling to complete the below pie chart. Use the information provided and complete the pie chart. The first segment has been drawn on for you.

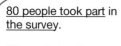

80 people took part in the survey.

35 people had brown eyes.

20 people had blue eyes.

15 people had green eyes.

10 people had hazel eyes.

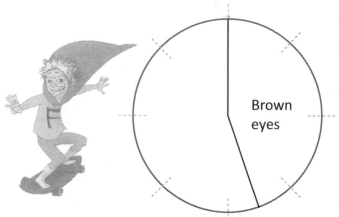

Brown eyes

Question 3

Favourite School Subject	Number of children
Maths	19
Science	11
English	27
History	21
Geography	13
P.E	9

SCHOOL SUBJECTS

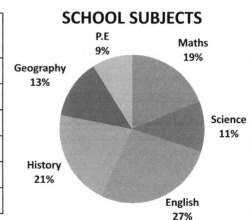

P.E 9%
Maths 19%
Geography 13%
Science 11%
History 21%
English 27%

a) What is the least favourite school subject?

b) How many people's favourite subjects were either History or Geography?

Question 4

Below is a diagram showing children's favourite zoo animals.

**40 CHILDREN WERE ASKED WHAT THEIR
FAVOURITE ANIMAL AT THE ZOO WAS**

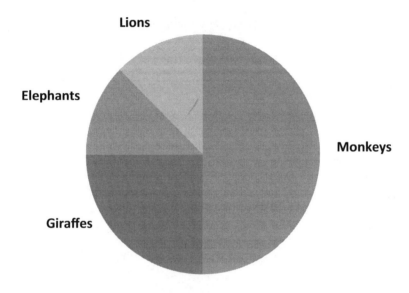

a) How many children chose giraffes?

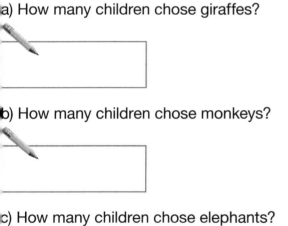

b) How many children chose monkeys?

c) How many children chose elephants?

d) How many more children chose monkeys over lions?

e) What was the second most popular animal?

Question 5

Using the above pie chart, if the survey was of 120 children, but the pie chart looked exactly the same, work out how many children would have said what answer.

a) Monkeys

b) Giraffes

c) Elephants

d) Lions

ANSWERS TO PIE CHARTS

Q1. a) False

EXPLANATION = Fizzy drinks are NOT more popular than fruit juice. Fizzy drinks was recorded as 27%, whereas fruit juice was recorded as 32%.

b) 10%

EXPLANATION = 10% of people chose smoothies as their favourite drink.

c) 19

EXPLANATION = if 100 people took part in the survey, and the percentage of people who chose milk as their favourite drink was 19%, that means 19 people out of 100 chose milk.

Q2. Your pie chart should look something like this:

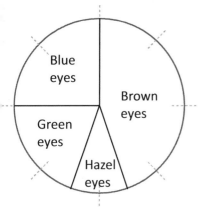

Q3. a) P.E

EXPLANATION = only 9 people chose P.E as their favourite subject. Therefore this is the least favourite subject.

b) 34

EXPLANATION = the number of people who chose History as their favourite subject = 21. The number of people who chose Geography as their favourite subject = 13. So, 21 + 13 = 34.

Q4. a) 10

b) 20

c) 5

d) 15

e) Giraffes

Q5. a) 60

b) 30

c) 15

d) 15

THE
REVISION
SERIES

LINE
GRAPHS

LINE GRAPHS

A line graph is used to represent data over a specific amount of time.

Instead of using bars like a bar chart, a line graph uses lines by plotting on the points and drawing a line through each of these points.

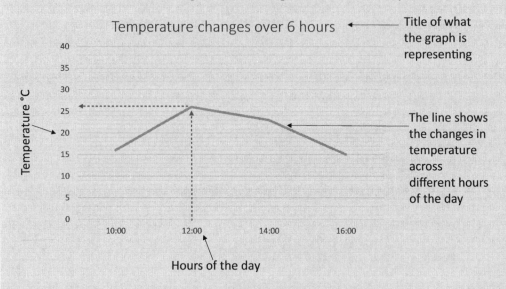

Work out the temperature at 12:00

Step 1 = draw an arrow from 12:00 all the way until you reach the line.

Step 2 = then read along that line and see what number it is.

Step 3 = the answer is 26 °C .

Now you try!

What was the approximate time when the temperature reached 20°C?

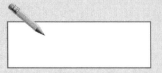

How much did the temperature increase from 10:00 to 12:00?

Question 1

Lalita needs your help. The data below shows the temperature changes across a day. Using the data provided, draw a line graph to illustrate the temperatures at these times.

TIME	TEMPERATURES
05:00	-4°C
07:00	1°C
09:00	7°C
11:00	10°C
13:00	11°C
15:00	13°C
17:00	12°C

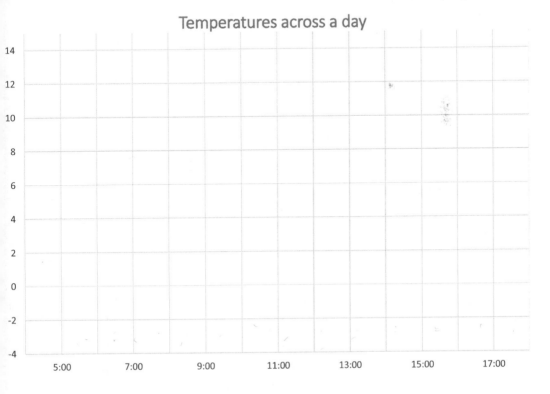

Temperatures across a day

Question 2

Below is a line graph showing the amount of rainfall (in millimetres) across several hours of a day.

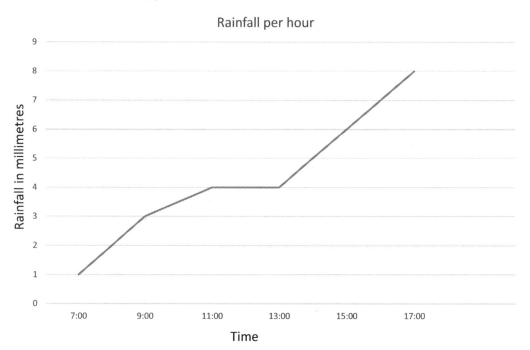

a) How much rain had fallen at 09:00?

b) What was the approximate rainfall at 14:00?

c) The amount of rainfall increased between the hours of 11:00 and 13:00. True or false?

Question 3

The below graph shows the weight of a baby from birth to 15 months.

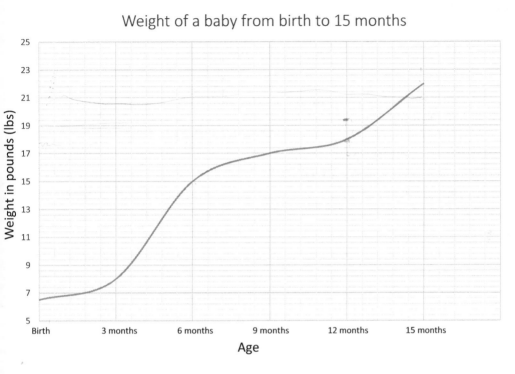

Weight of a baby from birth to 15 months

a) What is the weight of the baby aged 6 months?

b) If the baby loses 2 pounds at age 18 months, how much would the baby weigh?

c) How much weight did the baby gain from 6 months old to 12 months old?

Question 4

Below is Freddie's travelled distance.

> **Freddie's travelled distance**
>
> Begin at 0,0.
> In 10 minutes he travels 5 km.
> In 20 minutes he travels 18 km.
> In 30 minutes he travels 42 km.
> In 40 minutes he travels 60 km.
> In 50 minutes he travels 72 km.
> In 60 minutes he travels 94 km.

a) Using the information provided, draw this data on the line graph below.

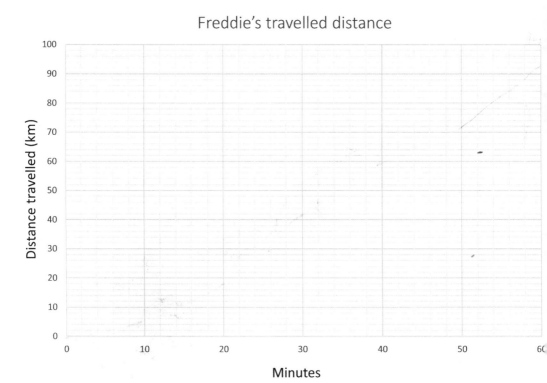

Freddie's travelled distance

b) How many minutes does it take Freddie to travel 60 km?

c) How many more kilometres did Freddie travel in 50 minutes as opposed to 20 minutes?

Question 5

Lalita and Scarlett both had winter colds. Their temperatures were recorded using the line graph below.

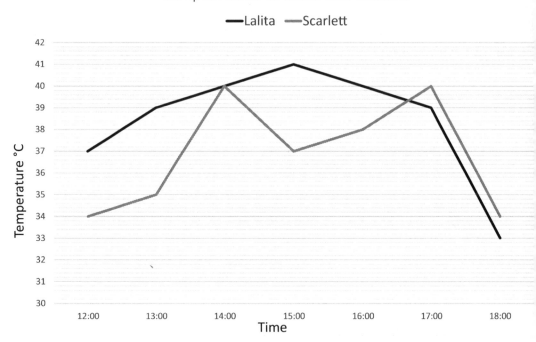

Temperatures of Lalita and Scarlett

—Lalita —Scarlett

a) What was the difference in Scarlett and Lalita's temperature at 15:00?

b) Who reached the highest temperature?

ANSWERS TO LINE GRAPHS

Q1. Your answer should look like this:

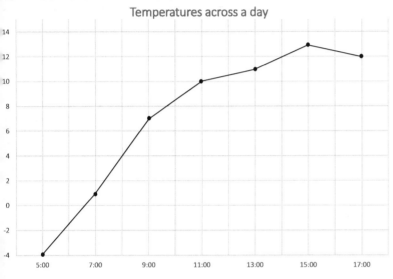

Temperatures across a day

Q2. a) 3 mm

EXPLANATION = at 09:00, it had rained 3 mm.

b) 5 mm

EXPLANATION = the approximate rainfall at 14:00 is 5 mm.

c) False

EXPLANATION = the rainfall between the hours of 11:00 and 13:00 did not increase; it stayed the same. Therefore this statement is false.

Q3. a) 15 lbs

EXPLANATION = at age 6 months, the baby weighed 15 lbs.

b) 20 lbs

EXPLANATION = if the baby loses 2 lbs at age 18 months, the baby would weigh 20 lbs.

22 lbs (at aged 15 months) – 2 lbs (loss of weight) = 20 lbs.

c) 3 lbs

EXPLANATION = the baby weighed 15 lbs at aged 6 months. The baby weighed 18 lbs at aged 12 months. Therefore the difference in weight is 3 lbs.

Q4. a) Your answer should look something like this:

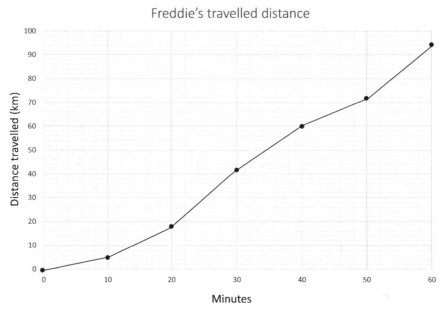

Freddie's travelled distance

b) 40 minutes

EXPLANATION = it takes Freddie 40 minutes to travel 60 kilometres.

c) 54 kilometres

EXPLANATION = Freddie travelled 72 kilometres in 50 minutes. He travelled 18 kilometres in 20 minutes. Therefore the difference in kilometres = 72 − 18 = 54 kilometres.

Q5. a) 4°C

EXPLANATION = Lalita's temperature at 15:00 was 41°C. Scarlett's temperature at 15:00 was 37°C. Therefore the difference in temperatures = 41 − 37 = 4°C.

b) Lalita

EXPLANATION = Lalita's temperature was recorded as the highest as it reached 41°C.

HOW ARE YOU GETTING ON?

THE
REVISION
SERIES

PICTOGRAMS

PICTOGRAMS

Pictograms are a FUN way of showing data.

Instead of using bars, lines or segments of pie, pictograms use pictures!

Example

Five people counted the number of balloons they popped in 30 seconds. Here are the results:

Preston 16   Freddie 19   Scarlett 9   Lalita 17   Anil 9

Instead of putting this data into a bar chart, you could represent it using pictures!

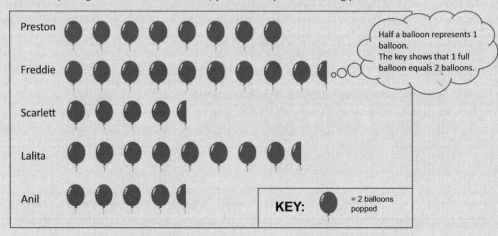

Half a balloon represents 1 balloon.
The key shows that 1 full balloon equals 2 balloons.

KEY: = 2 balloons popped

REMEMBER = the KEY is important! It tells you what each picture represents!

Now you try!

How many balloons did Freddie pop?

How many balloons were popped altogether?

Question 1

The pictogram below shows how many shooting stars Freddie saw across 12 months.

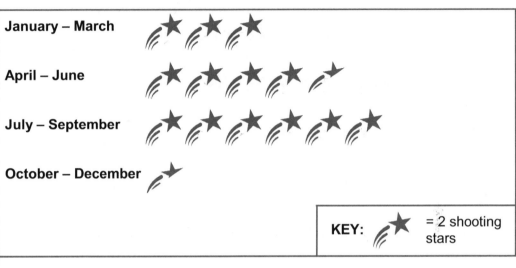

January – March

April – June

July – September

October – December

KEY: = 2 shooting stars

a) How many shooting stars did Freddie see between April and June?

b) On average, how many shooting stars did Freddie see per month, between January and March?

c) How many shooting stars did Freddie see altogether?

d) From January to March and July to September, what is the mean number of shooting stars Freddie saw?

Question 2

The pictogram below shows how many cars were spotted driving past Scarlett's house.

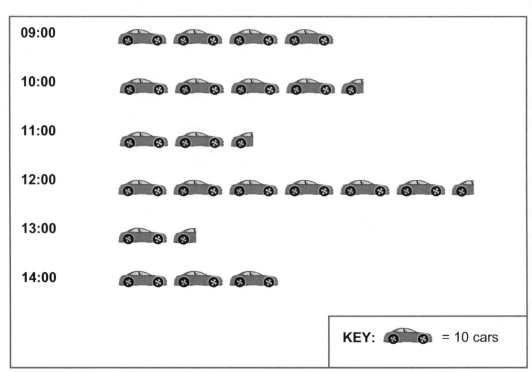

a) Which hour saw the least number of cars?

b) How many cars drove past Scarlett's house at 11:00?

c) How many fewer cars drove past at 13:00, compared to 10:00?

Question 3

a) Complete the pictogram using the data provided.

Favourite Ice Cream Flavour	Number of Children
Vanilla	9
Chocolate	14
Strawberry	4
Mint Chocolate	12
Rocky Road	2
Raspberry	7

Raspberry

Vanilla

Chocolate

Strawberry

KEY: = 2 children

b) How many people took part in this survey?

Question 4

The pictogram below shows how many crimes our superheroes have prevented.

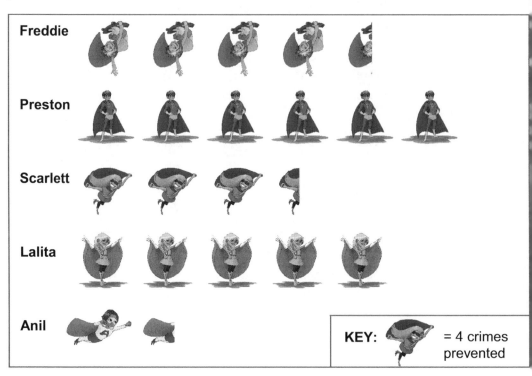

a) How many crimes did the girls prevent altogether?

b) How many crimes were prevented overall?

c) How many more crimes did Lalita prevent than Anil?

ANSWERS TO PICTOGRAMS

Q1. a) 9

  b) 2

  c) 28

  d) 3

Q2. a) 13:00

  b) 25

  c) 30

Q3. a) Your answer should look like this:

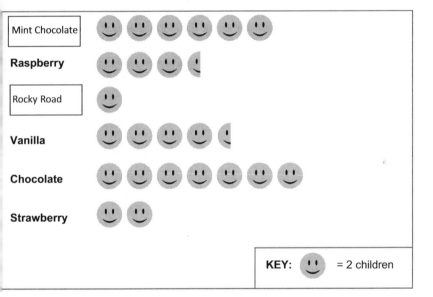

  b) 48

Q4. a) 34

  b) 82

  c) 14

THE
REVISION
SERIES

CARROLL
DIAGRAMS

CARROLL DIAGRAMS

Carroll diagrams are a useful way of sorting out information and arranging the data under the correct headings.

The use of Carroll diagrams allows you to categorise your data under specific headings.

5 9 27 35 15 10 18 54 36 30 20

	Multiples of 5	Multiples of 9
ODD	5 15 35	27 9
EVEN	10 30 20	36 54 18

TIP = cross off the numbers as you go. By crossing the numbers off as you go will make it easier to see what numbers you have put in the diagram already.

Now you try!

Put the following numbers under the correct subheadings of the diagram.

26 2 42 17 9 11 90 31 49 7 55

	Even	Odd
Prime Numbers		
Not Prime		

Question 1

Using the shapes below, draw them in the correct place of the Carroll diagram.

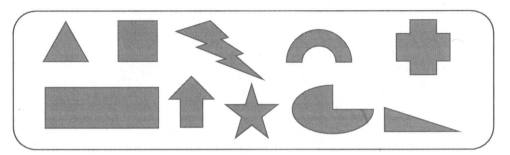

	Has no lines of symmetry	Has 1 or more lines of symmetry
Has 4 or less sides		
Has 5 or more sides		
Has a curved side		

Question 2

Complete the Carroll diagram using the information provided. Place the name of each person in the correct position.

> **Freddie** – Weight 53.5 kg, Height 165.1 cm
>
> **Preston** – Weight 52.6 kg, Height 167.6 cm
>
> **Scarlett** – Weight 48.5 kg, Height 170.2 cm
>
> **Lalita** – Weight 47.2 kg, Height 162.6 cm
>
> **Anil** – Weight 55.3 kg, Height 154.9 cm

	Weight 50 kg or less	Weight above 50 kg
Height 165 cm or less		
Height above 165 cm		

Question 3

Using the numbers listed below, place them in the correct part of the Carroll diagram.

7 41 28 25 40 77 3 13

	Multiples of 7	Not a multiple of 7
Less than 20		
More than 20		

Question 4

Using the numbers listed below, place them in the correct part of the Carroll diagram.

25 3 36 81 11 53 64 61

	Squared numbers	Prime numbers
Odd numbers		
Even numbers		

Question 5

Using the numbers listed below, place them in the correct part of the Carrol diagram.

| 1 | 21 | 17 | 16 | 47 | 24 | 4 | 38 |

	Between 10 and 20	Not between 10 and 20
Odd numbers		
Even numbers		

Question 6

Using the numbers listed below, place them in the correct part of the Carrol diagram.

| 8 | 5 | 6 | 18 | 10 | 12 | 20 | 9 |

	Factors of 36	Factors of 40
Numbers between 1 - 10		
Numbers between 11 - 20		

ANSWERS TO CARROLL DIAGRAMS

Q1. Your answer should look like this:

	Has no lines of symmetry	Has 1 or more lines of symmetry
Has 4 or less sides		
Has 5 or more sides		
Has a curved side		

Q2. Your answer should look like this:

	Weight 50 kg or less	Weight above 50 kg
Height 165 cm or less	Lalita	Anil
Height above 165 cm	Scarlett	Freddie Preston

Q3. Your answer should look like this:

	Multiples of 7	Not a multiple of 7
Less than 20	7	3 13
More than 20	28 77	41 25 40

Q4. Your answer should look like this:

	Squared numbers	Prime numbers
Odd numbers	25 81	3 11 53 61
Even numbers	36 64	

Q5. Your answer should look like this:

	Between 10 and 20	Not between 10 and 20
Odd numbers	17	1 21 47
Even numbers	16	24 4 38

Q6. Your answer should look like this:

	Factors of 36	Factors of 40
Numbers between 1 - 10	6 9	8 5 10
Numbers between 11 - 20	18 12	20

HOW ARE YOU GETTING ON?

THE
REVISION
SERIES

VENN
DIAGRAMS

VENN DIAGRAMS

Similar to Carroll diagrams, Venn diagrams are another way of **categorising** data by placing them under the correct headings.

The main difference between a Carroll diagram and a Venn diagram is that a Venn diagram has a part that **overlaps**, which means data can overlap with multiple categories.

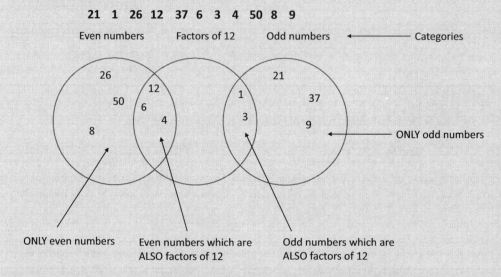

REMEMBER = be careful when placing the numbers under categories. Does the number apply to more than one category?

Now you try!

Use the numbers below and fill in the Venn diagram.

5   12   21   30   10   60   3   15

Multiples of 3   Multiples of 5

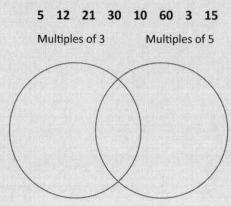

Question 1

Below is a Venn diagram. Using the data provided, fill in the Venn diagram.

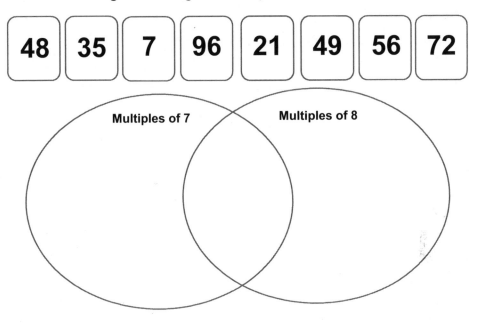

48 35 7 96 21 49 56 72

Multiples of 7   Multiples of 8

Question 2

Below is a Venn diagram. Using the data provided, fill in the Venn diagram.

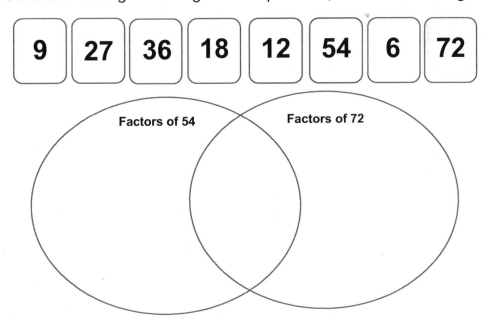

9 27 36 18 12 54 6 72

Factors of 54   Factors of 72

Question 3

a) Below is a Venn diagram. Using the data provided, fill in the Venn diagram.

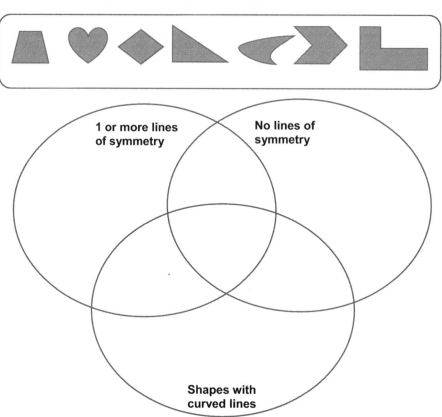

b) Draw the shape that has four lines of symmetry.

c) Which of the above shapes has a right angle? Draw the shape below.

Question 4

Below is a Venn diagram showing what children had in their lunch boxes.

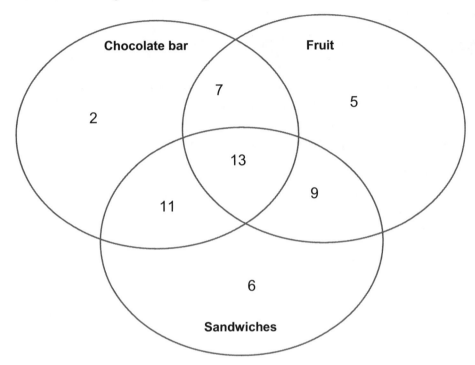

a) How many people had sandwiches and fruit in their lunch boxes?

b) How many people had a chocolate bar and a piece of fruit in their lunch boxes?

c) How many people took part in this study?

Question 5

Below is a Venn diagram. Using the data provided, fill in the Venn diagram.

| 20 | 12 | 40 | 33 | 52 | 27 | 2 | 24 |

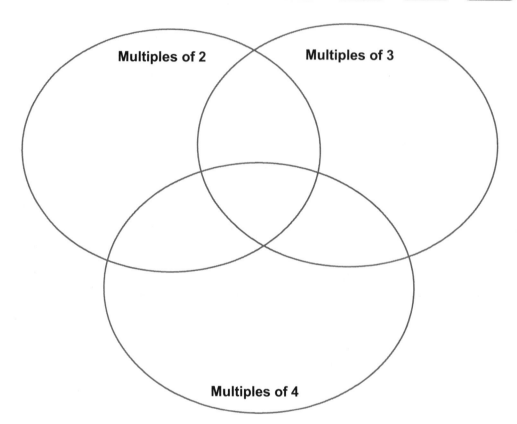

Question 6

Look at the Venn diagram and fill in the diagram with the information provided.

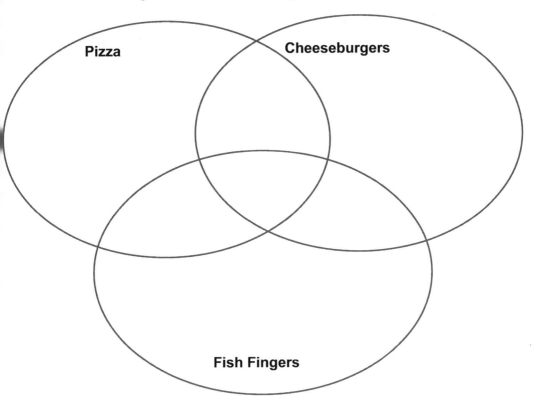

1) 5 children said they like pizza only.

2) 8 children said they like fish fingers and cheeseburgers.

3) 12 children said they like fish fingers and pizza.

4) 21 children said they like cheeseburgers only.

5) 15 children said they like fish fingers only.

6) 9 children said they like pizza, cheeseburgers and fish fingers.

7) 31 children said they like pizza and cheeseburgers.

ANSWERS TO VENN DIAGRAMS

Q1. Your answer should look like this:

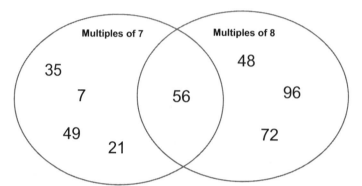

Multiples of 7 — 35, 7, 49, 21
56
Multiples of 8 — 48, 96, 72

Q2. Your answer should look like this:

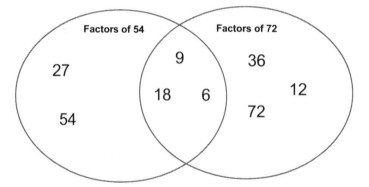

Factors of 54 — 27, 54
9, 18, 6
Factors of 72 — 36, 12, 72

Q3. a) Your answer should look like this:

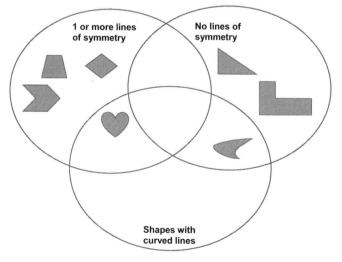

1 or more lines of symmetry

No lines of symmetry

Shapes with curved lines

b)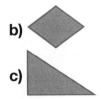

c)

Q4. a) 9

b) 7

c) 53

Q5. Your answer should look like this:

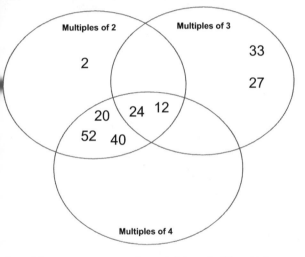

Q6. Your answer should look like this:

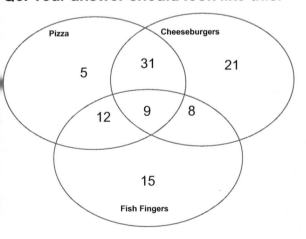

HOW ARE YOU GETTING ON?